EMMANUEL JOSEPH

Constellations of the Mind, A Journey Through Astronomy, Literature, and Human Emotion

Copyright © 2025 by Emmanuel Joseph

All rights reserved. No part of this publication may be reproduced, stored or transmitted in any form or by any means, electronic, mechanical, photocopying, recording, scanning, or otherwise without written permission from the publisher. It is illegal to copy this book, post it to a website, or distribute it by any other means without permission.

First edition

This book was professionally typeset on Reedsy.
Find out more at reedsy.com

Contents

1	Chapter 1: The Cosmic Perspective	1
2	Chapter 2: The Mythological Origins	3
3	Chapter 3: Literary Constellations	5
4	Chapter 4: Emotional Landscapes	7
5	Chapter 5: Scientific Discoveries	9
6	Chapter 6: Cultural Significance	11
7	Chapter 7: The Language of the Stars	13
8	Chapter 8: The Evolution of Constellations	15
9	Chapter 9: The Impact of Technology	17
10	Chapter 10: Constellations in Art	19
11	Chapter 11: Personal Reflections	21
12	Chapter 12: The Future of Constellations	23
13	Chapter 13: The Intersection of Science and Art	25
14	Chapter 14: Constellations and Human Connection	27
15	Chapter 15: The Journey Continues	29

1

Chapter 1: The Cosmic Perspective

The night sky has fascinated humans for millennia, serving as both a guide and a muse. From the earliest stargazers to modern astronomers, the stars have held a special place in our collective imagination. The constellations, in particular, have been a source of wonder and inspiration, forming intricate patterns that tell stories of gods, heroes, and mythical creatures. These celestial formations have not only guided sailors across uncharted waters but have also sparked the creative minds of poets and writers, who have woven their own tales of adventure and mystery.

Beyond their aesthetic beauty, the constellations offer a profound connection to the universe. Each star within a constellation is a distant sun, a reminder of the vastness of space and the incredible diversity of celestial bodies. The study of these stars has revealed much about the nature of our universe, from the life cycles of stars to the presence of exoplanets orbiting distant suns. As we gaze upon the constellations, we are reminded of our place in the cosmos and the shared history of stargazers who have come before us.

In literature, the constellations have been used as powerful symbols and metaphors, representing everything from destiny and fate to love and longing. The ancient Greeks, for example, saw the constellations as immortalized versions of their myths, with each star serving as a testament to the enduring power of storytelling. In more recent times, authors like John Milton and

William Blake have drawn upon the imagery of the stars to explore themes of light and darkness, knowledge and ignorance, and the eternal struggle between good and evil.

Emotionally, the constellations evoke a sense of awe and wonder, as well as a longing for connection and understanding. When we look up at the night sky, we are reminded of the mysteries that lie beyond our comprehension, and the endless possibilities that await us in the cosmos. This sense of wonder is deeply ingrained in the human psyche, driving us to explore, discover, and create. Whether through the lens of a telescope or the pages of a book, the constellations continue to inspire and captivate us, reminding us of the beauty and complexity of the universe we inhabit.

2

Chapter 2: The Mythological Origins

The origins of the constellations are deeply rooted in mythology, with cultures around the world creating their own celestial maps to explain the mysteries of the night sky. These mythological stories often reflect the values, beliefs, and experiences of the societies that created them, offering a unique window into the human condition. The Greek and Roman constellations, for example, are rich with tales of gods, heroes, and legendary creatures, each with its own unique story and significance.

One of the most famous constellations, Orion, tells the story of a mighty hunter who was placed among the stars by the gods. According to the myth, Orion was a giant of great strength and skill, whose adventures included slaying fearsome beasts and protecting the innocent. His tragic death, however, came at the hands of a scorpion sent by the goddess Artemis, leading to his eternal place in the heavens. The constellation of Orion, with its distinctive belt of three stars, serves as a reminder of both the heroism and vulnerability of the human spirit.

In Native American cultures, the constellations are often linked to the natural world and the cycles of life. The Big Dipper, for example, is known as the Great Bear in many Native American traditions, symbolizing strength, endurance, and the changing seasons. The stories associated with these constellations often emphasize the interconnectedness of all living things and the importance of living in harmony with nature. These narratives reflect a deep respect for the environment and a recognition of the delicate balance that sustains life on Earth.

Across the globe, the constellations have also been used as tools for navigation and timekeeping. In ancient Polynesia, skilled navigators relied on the stars to guide their voyages across vast expanses of the Pacific Ocean. The constellations served as a celestial compass, with specific stars and star patterns marking key points along their journey. This knowledge was passed down through generations, preserving the navigational traditions that allowed these seafaring cultures to explore and settle distant islands.

The mythological origins of the constellations remind us of the power of storytelling and its ability to connect us to the past, present, and future. These stories have been passed down through generations, evolving and adapting to reflect the changing world around us. As we continue to explore the cosmos and uncover new mysteries, the constellations serve as a timeless link to the myths and legends that have shaped our understanding of the universe.

3

Chapter 3: Literary Constellations

Literature has long been inspired by the constellations, with writers drawing upon the imagery and symbolism of the stars to explore a wide range of themes and emotions. From the epic tales of ancient Greece to the lyrical poetry of the Romantic era, the constellations have served as a rich source of inspiration for authors across time and cultures. These literary works not only reflect the beauty and mystery of the night sky but also offer insights into the human experience.

In Homer's "The Iliad" and "The Odyssey," the constellations play a crucial role in the journeys of heroes like Odysseus and Achilles. The stars serve as navigational aids, guiding the characters through treacherous seas and unknown lands. The constellations also symbolize the gods' influence over human fate, with characters often looking to the heavens for signs and omens. These epic tales highlight the enduring connection between the cosmos and the human quest for adventure, knowledge, and meaning.

The Romantic poets, including William Wordsworth and Samuel Taylor Coleridge, often used the constellations as symbols of beauty, inspiration, and transcendence. In their works, the stars evoke a sense of wonder and awe, reflecting the poets' deep appreciation for the natural world and their desire to connect with the divine. The constellations also serve as metaphors for the poets' inner emotional landscapes, representing their hopes, dreams, and struggles. Through their lyrical expressions, the Romantic poets remind us of the profound impact that the night sky can have on our hearts and minds.

In contemporary literature, the constellations continue to inspire authors in new and innovative ways. Science fiction writers, for example, often explore the possibilities of space travel and interstellar exploration, using the stars as a backdrop for their imaginative tales. These stories not only entertain but also provoke thought about the future of humanity and our place in the cosmos. The constellations, with their timeless beauty and mystery, provide a rich canvas for writers to explore the boundaries of human knowledge and creativity.

The literary constellations remind us of the enduring power of the written word and its ability to capture the wonder and complexity of the universe. Through the works of poets, novelists, and storytellers, the stars come alive with meaning and significance, offering a glimpse into the human soul. As we continue to gaze upon the night sky, we are reminded of the countless stories that have been inspired by the constellations and the infinite possibilities that lie ahead.

4

Chapter 4: Emotional Landscapes

The constellations have a unique ability to evoke a wide range of emotions, from awe and wonder to nostalgia and longing. As we gaze upon the stars, we are often reminded of our own experiences, dreams, and desires, creating a deeply personal connection to the cosmos. This emotional resonance is reflected in the art, literature, and music inspired by the constellations, capturing the profound impact that the night sky has on the human psyche.

In the realm of visual art, the constellations have been depicted in various forms, from detailed astronomical charts to imaginative celestial landscapes. Artists like Vincent van Gogh and Georgia O'Keeffe have drawn inspiration from the stars, using their unique styles to convey the beauty and mystery of the night sky. These works often evoke a sense of wonder and contemplation, inviting viewers to explore their own emotional landscapes and connect with the cosmos on a deeper level.

Music, too, has been influenced by the constellations, with composers and musicians drawing upon the imagery of the stars to create evocative and emotional pieces. Gustav Holst's "The Planets" is a prime example, with each movement representing a different celestial body and its associated astrological characteristics. The music captures the majesty and grandeur of the cosmos, transporting listeners to a world beyond our own. The constellations, with their timeless beauty, continue to inspire musicians to explore the emotional depths of the human experience.

In literature, the constellations often serve as symbols of longing, memory, and the passage of time. The stars are frequently used to represent lost loved ones, distant dreams, and the fleeting nature of life. In works like F. Scott Fitzgerald's "The Great Gatsby," the green light at the end of Daisy's dock becomes a symbol of Gatsby's unattainable dreams, much like a distant star shining in the night sky. The constellations remind us of the impermanence of our own existence and the enduring nature of the universe, offering a poignant reflection on the human condition.

The emotional landscapes inspired by the constellations are a testament to their enduring power and significance. As we continue to explore the mysteries of the cosmos, we are reminded of the deep connection between the stars and our own inner worlds. Whether through art, music, or literature, the constellations provide a timeless source of inspiration, evoking emotions that transcend time and space. They remind us of the beauty and complexity of the universe and our place within it, offering a sense of wonder and hope as we navigate our own journeys.

5

Chapter 5: Scientific Discoveries

The study of the constellations has led to countless scientific discoveries, revealing the inner workings of the universe and expanding our understanding of the cosmos. From the earliest observations of ancient astronomers to the cutting-edge research of modern scientists, the constellations have played a crucial role in the advancement of astronomy. These discoveries have not only deepened our knowledge of the stars but have also shed light on the fundamental principles that govern the universe.

One of the most significant discoveries in the history of astronomy was the realization that the Earth is not the center of the universe. The heliocentric model, proposed by Copernicus and later supported by Galileo and Kepler, challenged the long-held belief that the Earth was stationary and at the center of all celestial motion. This paradigm shift was monumental, paving the way for a more accurate understanding of the cosmos and our place within it. The constellations, once seen as fixed and immutable, became part of a dynamic and ever-changing universe.

The study of the constellations has also led to the discovery of new celestial bodies and phenomena. The invention of the telescope in the early 17th century allowed astronomers to observe the night sky in unprecedented detail, revealing the existence of previously unseen stars, planets, and moons. Galileo's observations of the moons of Jupiter, for example, provided concrete evidence that not all celestial bodies orbit the Earth. These discoveries expanded our understanding of the solar system and demonstrated the vast diversity of celestial objects.

In the modern era, advancements in technology and space exploration have taken our study of the constellations to new heights. The Hubble Space Telescope, launched in 1990, has provided breathtaking images of distant galaxies, nebulae, and star clusters, offering a glimpse into the farthest reaches of the universe. These observations have revealed the presence of exoplanets, black holes, and other phenomena that were once only theoretical. The constellations, once viewed solely from the ground, are now explored through the lens of cutting-edge technology.

The scientific discoveries made through the study of the constellations have profound implications for our understanding of the universe and our place within it. They remind us of the boundless curiosity and ingenuity that drive human exploration and discovery. As we continue to explore the cosmos, the constellations serve as a constant source of inspiration and a reminder of the endless possibilities that lie ahead.

6

Chapter 6: Cultural Significance

The constellations hold deep cultural significance for societies around the world, reflecting the values, beliefs, and traditions of diverse cultures. These celestial patterns have been used to mark important events, guide agricultural practices, and serve as symbols in religious and spiritual rituals. The cultural significance of the constellations offers a unique insight into the ways in which different societies have understood and interacted with the night sky.

In ancient Egypt, the constellations played a crucial role in the development of the calendar and the timing of agricultural activities. The heliacal rising of the star Sirius, for example, marked the beginning of the annual flooding of the Nile River, which was essential for the fertility of the land. The constellations were also incorporated into the design of temples and pyramids, aligning with specific stars and celestial events to symbolize the connection between the heavens and the earthly realm.

In Chinese culture, the constellations are an integral part of traditional astronomy and astrology. The Chinese sky is divided into 28 lunar mansions, each associated with specific stars and constellations. These mansions serve as markers for the moon's path and are used to predict celestial events and their influence on human affairs. The constellations are also linked to mythology and folklore, with each star and star cluster representing gods, heroes, and mythical creatures. The cultural significance of the constellations in Chinese tradition reflects the deep connection between the cosmos and the natural and human worlds.

In the Indigenous cultures of Australia, the constellations hold profound spiritual and cultural significance. The night sky is viewed as a canvas for ancestral stories and Dreamtime myths, with each constellation representing a specific narrative or lesson. The Emu in the Sky, for example, is a dark constellation formed by the dark patches of the Milky Way, symbolizing the emu, a sacred bird in many Indigenous Australian cultures. These stories are passed down through generations, preserving the cultural heritage and wisdom of the community.

The cultural significance of the constellations highlights the diverse ways in which different societies have interpreted and understood the night sky. These celestial patterns serve as a bridge between the heavens and the earth, connecting us to our ancestors, traditions, and the natural world. As we continue to explore the cosmos, we are reminded of the rich cultural tapestry that the constellations represent and the enduring legacy of human curiosity and creativity.

7

Chapter 7: The Language of the Stars

The constellations have their own language, a system of symbols and meanings that have been used to convey information and tell stories for millennia. This language of the stars is a universal form of communication, transcending cultural and temporal boundaries. By understanding the symbols and patterns of the constellations, we can unlock the wisdom and knowledge embedded in the night sky.

In ancient Greece, the constellations were named after gods, heroes, and mythical creatures, each with its own unique story and symbolism. The constellation of Andromeda, for example, represents the princess who was chained to a rock as a sacrifice to a sea monster but was ultimately saved by the hero Perseus. This mythological tale is encoded in the stars, serving as a reminder of themes such as bravery, sacrifice, and redemption. The language of the stars in Greek mythology is a rich tapestry of interconnected stories that reflect the values and beliefs of the culture.

In medieval Europe, the constellations were incorporated into the practice of astrology, with each star sign representing specific personality traits and destinies. The zodiac, a belt of constellations along the ecliptic, became a tool for divination and self-discovery. Each zodiac sign has its own associated symbol, element, and ruling planet, creating a complex system of meanings that astrologers use to interpret the influence of the stars on human affairs. The language of the stars in astrology offers insights into the human psyche and the interconnectedness of the cosmos and individual lives.

In the Islamic world, the study of the constellations was advanced by astronomers who created detailed star maps and cataloged celestial objects. The language of the stars in Islamic astronomy is one of precision and scientific inquiry, reflecting the culture's emphasis on observation and mathematical calculations. The constellations were used to determine the direction of Mecca for prayer, mark the timing of religious festivals, and guide travelers across vast deserts. The language of the stars in Islamic tradition is a testament to the culture's contributions to the field of astronomy and its deep connection to the night sky.

The language of the stars is a powerful form of communication that has been used to convey information, tell stories, and explore the mysteries of the universe. By understanding this language, we can connect with the wisdom and knowledge of our ancestors and gain a deeper appreciation for the beauty and complexity of the cosmos. The constellations continue to speak to us, inviting us to explore their meanings and uncover the secrets of the night sky.

8

Chapter 8: The Evolution of Constellations

The constellations have not always been the same as we see them today. Over time, the stars that make up these celestial patterns have shifted, and new constellations have been added to the night sky. The evolution of the constellations reflects the dynamic nature of the universe and the ever-changing human understanding of the cosmos.

In ancient times, the constellations were often based on the myths and legends of the culture that created them. The ancient Greeks, for example, developed a system of constellations that reflected their mythology and worldview. As these stories were passed down through generations, the constellations became an integral part of their cultural heritage. However, as new cultures emerged and exchanged ideas, the constellations evolved to incorporate new myths and stories.

The Age of Exploration in the 15th and 16th centuries brought about a significant expansion of the known constellations. European explorers and navigators, traveling to previously uncharted regions of the world, encountered new stars and celestial patterns that were not visible from their homelands. These discoveries were incorporated into the existing system of constellations, resulting in a more comprehensive and diverse celestial map. The constellations of the Southern Hemisphere, such as the Southern Cross and Carina, became part of the global celestial heritage.

In the modern era, the International Astronomical Union (IAU) established a standardized system of 88 constellations that are recognized worldwide. This system, adopted in 1922, provides a consistent framework for identifying and studying the stars. The IAU constellations are based on both ancient and modern traditions, reflecting the diverse cultural contributions to our understanding of the night sky. This standardized system has facilitated collaboration and communication among astronomers and has helped to preserve the rich history of celestial mapping.

The evolution of the constellations is a testament to the dynamic nature of human knowledge and our ever-expanding understanding of the universe. As we continue to explore the cosmos and make new discoveries, the constellations will undoubtedly continue to evolve. These celestial patterns serve as a reminder of our shared history and the enduring curiosity that drives us to explore the mysteries of the night sky. The constellations are not static; they are living symbols of our quest for knowledge and understanding.

9

Chapter 9: The Impact of Technology

The advancement of technology has revolutionized our understanding of the constellations and the cosmos. From the invention of the telescope to the development of space probes and satellites, technology has enabled us to explore the universe in ways that were once unimaginable. The impact of technology on the study of the constellations is profound, offering new insights and expanding our knowledge of the stars.

The invention of the telescope in the early 17th century revolutionized our understanding of the constellations and the cosmos. Galileo Galilei's observations of the moon, the planets, and the stars provided unprecedented insights into the nature of the universe. With the telescope, astronomers could observe celestial objects in greater detail, revealing the intricate structures of star clusters, nebulae, and galaxies. The telescope opened up new avenues of exploration, transforming the study of the constellations from a purely visual practice to a scientific discipline.

In the 20th century, advancements in technology continued to expand our knowledge of the constellations. The launch of space probes and satellites allowed astronomers to observe the stars from beyond the Earth's atmosphere, providing clearer and more detailed images of the cosmos. The Hubble Space Telescope, launched in 1990, has been instrumental in capturing stunning images of distant galaxies and nebulae, offering a glimpse into the farthest reaches of the universe. These observations have led to groundbreaking discoveries, such as the existence of exoplanets and the presence of dark matter.

The development of computer technology has also had a significant impact on the study of the constellations. Modern astronomers use sophisticated software and algorithms to analyze vast amounts of data, uncovering patterns and relationships that were previously hidden. These tools have enabled scientists to map the distribution of stars and galaxies, providing insights into the large-scale structure of the universe. The constellations, once viewed as isolated patterns of stars, are now understood as part of a dynamic and interconnected cosmic web.

As technology continues to advance, our understanding of the constellations and the cosmos will undoubtedly continue to evolve. The future promises new discoveries and deeper insights into the nature of the universe, driven by the relentless curiosity and ingenuity of humanity. The impact of technology on the study of the constellations is a testament to the power of human innovation and the enduring quest for knowledge.

10

Chapter 10: Constellations in Art

The constellations have long been a source of inspiration for artists, who have drawn upon the imagery and symbolism of the stars to create captivating works of art. From ancient star maps to contemporary installations, the constellations have been depicted in various forms, reflecting the beauty and mystery of the night sky. These artistic representations offer a unique perspective on the constellations, capturing the imagination and evoking a sense of wonder.

In ancient times, the constellations were often depicted in detailed star maps and celestial globes, which served both practical and artistic purposes. These maps were used by astronomers to navigate the night sky and track the movements of celestial bodies, while also serving as decorative objects that celebrated the beauty of the stars. The constellations were often illustrated with intricate designs and mythological figures, highlighting the cultural significance of these celestial patterns.

During the Renaissance, artists such as Albrecht Dürer and Johannes Hevelius created elaborate star atlases that combined scientific observation with artistic expression. These atlases featured detailed engravings of the constellations, accompanied by descriptions of their mythological origins and astronomical properties. The fusion of art and science in these works reflects the Renaissance ideal of the "universal man," who sought to integrate knowledge from diverse fields.

In the modern era, artists continue to be inspired by the constellations, exploring their symbolism and meaning through various media. The contemporary artist Yayoi Kusama, for example, has created immersive installations that evoke the sensation of being surrounded by stars. Her "Infinity Mirror Rooms" use mirrors and LED lights to create a mesmerizing and infinite expanse, capturing the boundless nature of the cosmos. These installations invite viewers to contemplate their place in the universe and the interconnectedness of all things.

The constellations also feature prominently in public art and architecture, with many cities around the world incorporating celestial motifs into their design. The Griffith Observatory in Los Angeles, for example, features a stunning mural of the constellations on its ceiling, providing a visual representation of the night sky. These artistic depictions of the constellations serve as a reminder of the beauty and wonder of the cosmos, inspiring both residents and visitors to look up and explore the mysteries of the universe.

11

Chapter 11: Personal Reflections

The constellations have a unique ability to evoke personal reflections and introspection, inviting us to explore our own thoughts, feelings, and experiences. As we gaze upon the stars, we are often reminded of the moments in our lives that have shaped us, the dreams we hold dear, and the connections we share with others. The constellations serve as a mirror to our inner world, reflecting the emotions and memories that define us.

For many, the constellations are a source of comfort and solace, providing a sense of continuity and stability in an ever-changing world. The stars remain constant and unchanging, a reliable presence in the night sky that has been witnessed by countless generations. This sense of permanence can be reassuring, offering a reminder that we are part of something larger and more enduring than ourselves. The constellations invite us to find peace and perspective in the midst of life's challenges.

The constellations also serve as a canvas for our dreams and aspirations, encouraging us to reach for the stars and pursue our goals. Throughout history, the stars have been associated with ambition and achievement, symbolizing the limitless potential of the human spirit. The constellation of Hercules, for example, represents the hero who accomplished seemingly impossible tasks through determination and perseverance. The constellations inspire us to believe in ourselves and strive for greatness, no matter how daunting the journey may seem.

In moments of reflection, the constellations remind us of the connections we share with others, both past and present. The stories and myths associated with the stars have been passed down through generations, creating a sense of continuity and shared heritage. As we look up at the same stars that our ancestors once gazed upon, we are reminded of the enduring bonds that unite us. The constellations invite us to connect with others, to share our stories, and to find meaning in the shared experience of being human.

The personal reflections inspired by the constellations are a testament to their enduring power and significance. As we continue to explore the mysteries of the cosmos, we are reminded of the deep connection between the stars and our own inner worlds. The constellations invite us to look within, to explore our thoughts and feelings, and to find meaning and inspiration in the beauty of the night sky.

12

Chapter 12: The Future of Constellations

As we look to the future, the constellations will continue to play a significant role in our exploration and understanding of the cosmos. Advances in technology, new discoveries, and the ongoing quest for knowledge will shape the way we perceive and interact with the constellations. The future of constellations promises exciting possibilities and new opportunities for discovery.

One of the most promising areas of future exploration is the study of exoplanets, planets that orbit stars outside our solar system. The constellations serve as a guide for astronomers searching for these distant worlds, with many exoplanets being located within specific star systems. Future missions, such as the James Webb Space Telescope, will provide unprecedented insights into the nature of exoplanets and their potential for habitability. The constellations will continue to be a focal point for our search for life beyond Earth.

Advancements in space travel and exploration will also expand our understanding of the constellations. Future missions to the moon, Mars, and beyond will provide new perspectives on the night sky, allowing us to observe the stars from different vantage points. The constellations will serve as a guide for these journeys, helping us navigate the cosmos and uncover new mysteries. As we venture further into space, the constellations will remain a constant and familiar presence, reminding us of our connection to the universe.

In addition to scientific exploration, the constellations will continue to inspire art, literature, and culture. New generations of artists, writers, and musicians will draw upon the imagery and symbolism of the stars to create works that reflect the evolving human experience. The constellations will serve as a timeless source of inspiration, connecting us to the past while guiding us toward the future. As we continue to explore the cosmos, the constellations will remain a beacon of creativity and imagination.

The future of the constellations is bright, filled with endless possibilities for discovery and exploration. As we continue to gaze upon the night sky, we are reminded of the enduring power of the stars to inspire, captivate, and connect us. The constellations invite us to embark on a journey of discovery, to explore the mysteries of the universe, and to find meaning and wonder in the beauty of the night sky. The constellations are a testament to the boundless curiosity and ingenuity of humanity, a reminder that the journey is far from over.

13

Chapter 13: The Intersection of Science and Art

The intersection of science and art is beautifully exemplified by the constellations. As scientific understanding of the stars has advanced, artists have continued to find new ways to interpret and represent these celestial patterns. This convergence of disciplines has enriched both fields, leading to a deeper appreciation of the cosmos and the creative process.

In the Renaissance, the works of Leonardo da Vinci and other polymaths bridged the gap between science and art. Da Vinci's sketches of celestial objects, based on his observations and studies, demonstrated a profound understanding of both the artistic and scientific principles governing the stars. His ability to blend art and science inspired generations of artists and scientists alike, fostering a holistic approach to understanding the universe.

In the modern era, collaborations between scientists and artists have led to innovative projects that explore the beauty and complexity of the cosmos. The Cosmic Microwave Background (CMB) art project, for example, transformed data from the early universe into stunning visual representations, allowing people to see the intricate patterns of cosmic radiation. These projects not only make scientific concepts more accessible but also inspire a sense of wonder and curiosity.

The intersection of science and art continues to evolve, with new technologies enabling even more creative interpretations of the night sky. Digital art and virtual reality allow for immersive experiences that transport viewers to the farthest reaches of the universe. These artistic representations of the constellations inspire a deeper connection to the cosmos, reminding us of the endless possibilities that lie at the intersection of science and art.

14

Chapter 14: Constellations and Human Connection

The constellations have always played a role in fostering human connection, serving as a common reference point for people across time and cultures. Gazing at the night sky, individuals from different backgrounds and eras have shared the same sense of wonder and curiosity, creating a bond that transcends geographical and temporal boundaries.

In ancient times, the constellations were used as markers for important communal events, such as agricultural festivals and religious ceremonies. These gatherings fostered a sense of unity and shared purpose, as communities came together to celebrate the cycles of the heavens. The constellations served as a reminder of the interconnectedness of all living things and the importance of working together to sustain life.

In modern society, the constellations continue to bring people together, whether through stargazing clubs, planetarium shows, or public astronomical events. These activities provide opportunities for individuals to connect with one another and share their passion for the cosmos. The constellations serve as a focal point for discussions about science, culture, and the mysteries of the universe, fostering a sense of community and collaboration.

The constellations also play a role in personal relationships, with many people finding meaning and connection in shared stargazing experiences.

Couples often look to the stars as a symbol of their love and commitment, while families pass down stories and traditions related to the constellations. These shared experiences create lasting memories and strengthen the bonds between individuals, reminding us of the enduring power of the stars to bring people together.

15

Chapter 15: The Journey Continues

As we move forward into the future, the journey of exploration and discovery inspired by the constellations continues. The night sky remains a source of endless fascination, prompting us to ask questions, seek answers, and push the boundaries of our understanding. The constellations, with their timeless beauty and mystery, will continue to guide and inspire us on this journey.

Future generations will build upon the knowledge and discoveries of the past, using advanced technologies and innovative techniques to explore the cosmos in new ways. Missions to distant planets, the search for extraterrestrial life, and the study of dark matter and dark energy will expand our understanding of the universe and our place within it. The constellations will serve as a guide and inspiration for these endeavors, reminding us of the importance of curiosity, creativity, and collaboration.

The journey through the constellations is not just a scientific pursuit; it is also a personal and emotional one. As we gaze upon the stars, we are reminded of our own dreams, aspirations, and connections to others. The constellations invite us to reflect on our place in the universe and the ways in which we can contribute to the greater good. They inspire us to seek knowledge, embrace creativity, and nurture our relationships with one another.

Book Description

"Constellations of the Mind: A Journey Through Astronomy, Literature, and Human Emotion" explores the profound connection between the night sky and the human experience. This captivating book delves into the rich history of the constellations, from their mythological origins and cultural significance to their influence on art, literature, and scientific discovery. Each chapter offers a unique perspective on the stars, highlighting their role as symbols of beauty, inspiration, and transcendence.

Through a blend of storytelling, scientific insights, and personal reflections, "Constellations of the Mind" invites readers to embark on a journey of exploration and discovery. The book examines the timeless allure of the constellations, revealing the ways in which they have shaped human imagination and understanding. From the epic tales of ancient Greece to the innovative projects of modern artists and scientists, the constellations serve as a constant source of wonder and inspiration.

This book also explores the emotional landscapes inspired by the stars, capturing the awe, nostalgia, and longing that the night sky evokes. Through art, music, and literature, the constellations continue to touch our hearts and minds, offering a glimpse into the mysteries of the universe and our place within it. "Constellations of the Mind" is a celebration of the enduring power of the stars to captivate, inspire, and connect us, reminding us of the beauty and complexity of the cosmos we inhabit.

www.ingramcontent.com/pod-product-compliance
Lightning Source LLC
LaVergne TN
LVHW010443070526
838199LV00066B/6164